Electricity and Magnets

By Mary F. Blehl

Glenview, Illinois
Boston, Massachusetts
Chandler, Arizona
Upper Saddle River, New Jersey

Illustrations
FP2 Peter Bollinger.

Photographs
Every effort has been made to secure permission and provide appropriate credit for photographic material.
The publisher deeply regrets any omission and pledges to correct errors called to its attention in subsequent editions.

Unless otherwise acknowledged, all photographs are the copyright © of Dorling Kindersley, a division of Pearson.

Photo locators denoted as follows: Top (T), Center (C), Bottom (B), Left (L), Right (R), Background (Bkgd).

Opener: Rob Matheson/Corbis; 3 ©Rob Matheson/Corbis; 12 ©Erich Schrempp/Photo Researchers, Inc.; 21 (B) Science Photos/Alamy Images; 22 (TC) ©George Bernard/Photo Researchers, Inc., (TR, CR) ©Science Photo Library/Photo Researchers, Inc., (CR) ©DK Images, (BC) The Granger Collection, NY, (BR) Science & Society Picture Library.

FP2 (TCL) ©Berci/Shutterstock, (BCL) ©Cameron/Corbis, (TCR) ©Martin Bond/Photo Researchers, Inc., (BL) DK Images; FP3 (TR) ©Cameron/Corbis; FP4 (B) ©DK Images; FP5 (B) Andy Crawford/DK Images; FP6 (B) ©DK Images.

ISBN-13: 978-0-328-65781-0
ISBN-10:   0-328-65781-6

7 8 9 10 11 V0FL 17 16 15

Charged Matter

Atoms and Electric Charges

Maybe you have touched a door handle after you walked across a rug. Then you felt a pop of static electricity. Why did this happen?

To answer that question, we must look at what matter is made of. Everything is made of tiny particles called atoms.

Atoms are made of even smaller particles. Some particles have a positive charge. Some have a negative charge. Some particles have no charge at all. The number of positive and negative particles in an atom is usually equal.

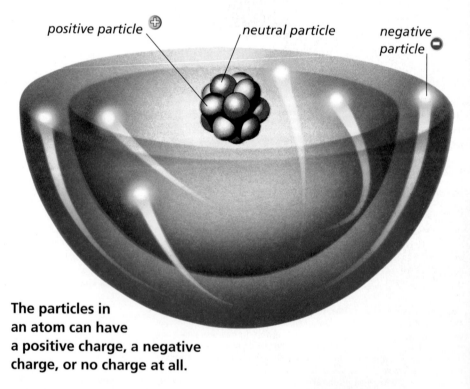

positive particle

neutral particle

negative particle

The particles in an atom can have a positive charge, a negative charge, or no charge at all.

Static Electricity

Charged particles can move from one object to another. When the positive and negative particles do not balance, it is called **static electricity.**

The word *static* means "not moving." When we talk about static electricity, we usually talk about one thing with a positive charge and one thing with a negative charge. Eventually the charges pile up and static electricity moves.

Lightning is also a kind of static electricity. Charged particles move between atoms in storm clouds. Positive particles usually pile up near the top of the clouds. Negative particles pile up near the bottom. This builds up static electricity. This energy is released as lightning.

Static electricity can build up in clouds. Then we see lightning.

Charged Objects

The movement of charged particles can be predicted. An object with a positive charge will be attracted to, or will pull toward, an object with a negative charge. This attraction is an electric force.

Think about why a balloon sticks to the wall after you rub it on your hair. When you rub the balloon, it might pick up some negative particles. Then the negative charge on the balloon is attracted to the positive charge on the wall. So the balloon sticks. Eventually the balloon loses the charge and drops to the ground.

Try rubbing balloons on your hair and then sticking them to your clothes!

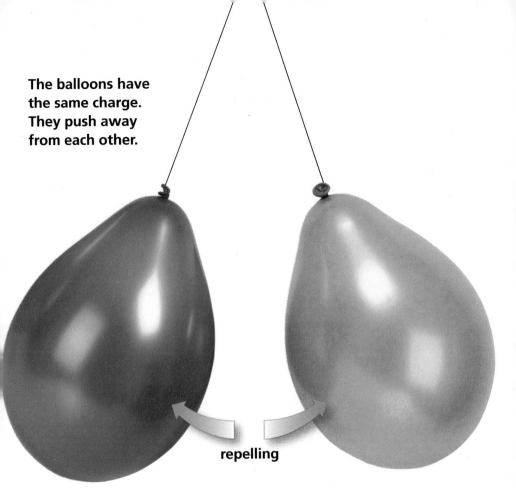

The balloons have the same charge. They push away from each other.

repelling

What if you rubbed two balloons on your hair? Would these balloons stick to each other? As you know, both balloons pick up negative particles from your hair. When you try to put these negatively charged balloons together, they will repel, or push away from, each other. Objects that have the same charge do not attract each other. Positive charges repel other positive charges, and negative charges repel other negative charges.

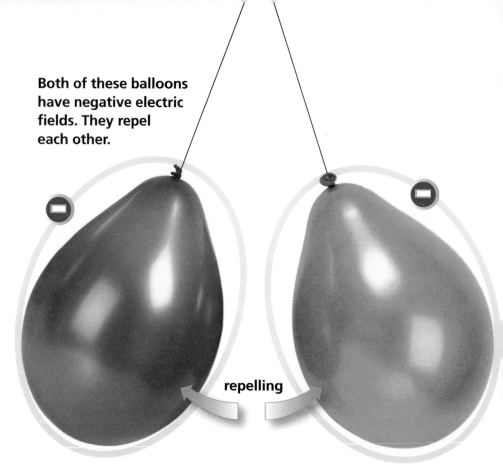

Both of these balloons have negative electric fields. They repel each other.

repelling

Electric Fields

The space around an object with an electric charge is called an electric field. Electric fields cannot be seen. Scientists show electric fields by drawing lines coming from an object. An electric field has the most strength when it is closest to a charged object. It loses strength as it gets farther away from the charged object.

Negative electric fields attract positively charged particles and matter. They repel negative particles. Positive electric fields attract negatively charged particles and matter. They repel positively charged particles.

Think of the balloons you read about earlier. After the balloons are rubbed on your hair, they each have negative electric fields around them. Since these fields have the same charge, they repel each other.

Suppose you rubbed only one of the balloons on your hair. That balloon would have a negative electric field around it. But the second balloon would not have this negative field. The two balloons would have opposite charges, and they would attract each other.

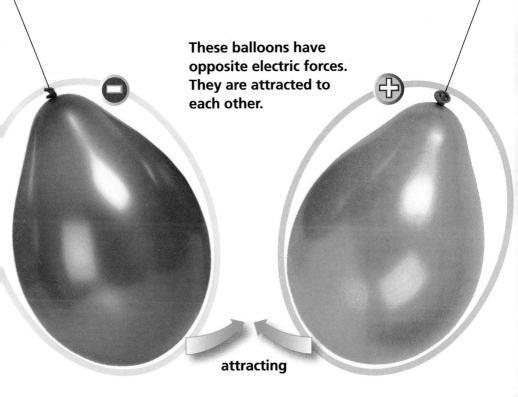

These balloons have opposite electric forces. They are attracted to each other.

attracting

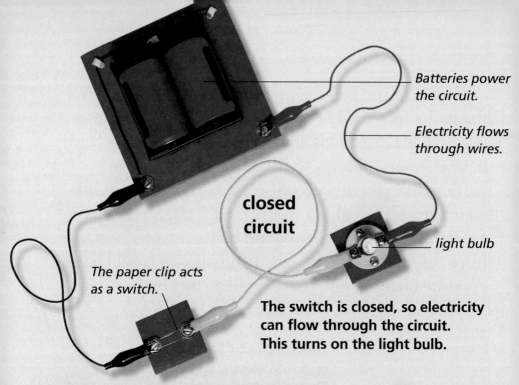

Batteries power the circuit.

Electricity flows through wires.

closed circuit

light bulb

The paper clip acts as a switch.

The switch is closed, so electricity can flow through the circuit. This turns on the light bulb.

The Movement Of Electric Charges

Electric Current

Static energy tends to stay in one place. But most electricity moves around. An **electric current** is an electric charge in motion. You cannot see an electric current.

Electric charges flow through a circuit. The circuit must be an unbroken loop in order for electricity to move through it. A circuit that has no breaks in it is a closed circuit. An open circuit has at least one break. This break keeps electric charges from flowing.

An electric charge does not flow the same way through all materials. A conductor is a material made of atoms that pick up charges easily. Many metals are good conductors. Some coins and spoons can conduct an electric charge very well.

Insulators are materials whose atoms do not pick up charges easily. This means they have **resistance.** An electric charge does not flow through insulators quickly. Wood, rubber, and plastic are good insulators. Metal wires are often covered with an insulator to keep electric charges from moving from wire to wire.

Which of these objects are conductors and which are insulators?

coin

metal spoon

eraser

wooden spoon

Series Circuits

An electric charge moves in one path in a **series circuit.** A power source is turned on, and charged particles move through a wire in a loop. Suppose there are several light bulbs along this wire. They will all get the same amount of energy.

Now suppose one bulb burns out. That breaks the circuit! When there is a break in the circuit, the electric charge will not flow to the next light. So even though only one bulb is burned out, none of them will give off light. All devices in a series circuit share electric current.

In a series circuit, if one light bulb goes out, all the light bulbs on the string go out.

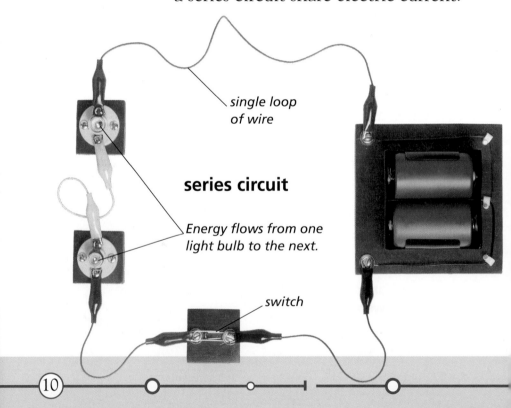

single loop
of wire

series circuit

Energy flows from one
light bulb to the next.

switch

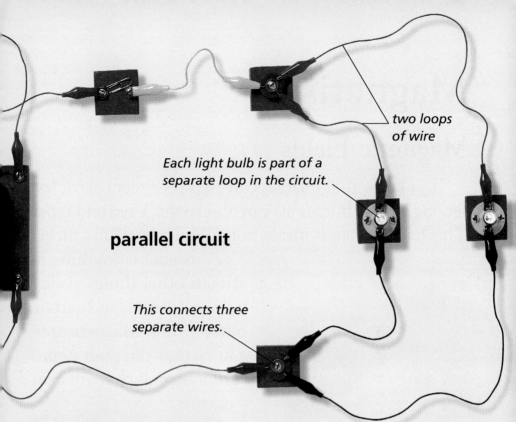

two loops
of wire

Each light bulb is part of a
separate loop in the circuit.

parallel circuit

This connects three
separate wires.

Parallel Circuits

A parallel circuit is different from a series circuit.
A **parallel circuit** has separate wires going to each
light bulb. Each wire also goes to the source of electricity.
Then if one bulb burns out, the others stay lit.

Look at the circuit above. You can see that each
bulb is connected directly to a separate loop of wires
in the circuit. The electricity flows through the wires
to the bulbs.

Your house and school have parallel circuits. This is
so that electricity can still flow if there is a break in one
part of the circuit.

Magnetism

Magnetic Fields

You know that charges can attract or repel particles among atoms. But atoms can also be attracted and repelled. This happens often inside iron, cobalt, steel, and nickel.

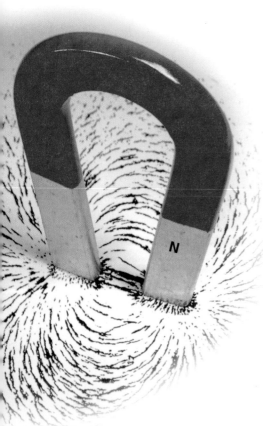

A magnet is anything that attracts other things made from iron, steel, and certain other metals. **Magnetism** is a force that can push or pull certain metals that are near a magnet.

Magnets are surrounded by an invisible field. This field of attraction is a magnetic field. A **magnetic field** is the place around a magnet where the force of magnetism can be felt. The shape of a magnetic field depends on the shape of the magnet.

A magnet can pull iron filings toward itself, making a pattern such as the one you see here. The **N** stands for the north pole of the magnet.

Magnetic Poles

These iron filings show the field of attraction between the opposite poles of two magnets.

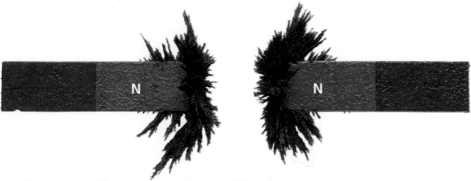

These iron filings show the repelling force between like poles of two magnets.

Magnets have two poles. One is called north, and one is called south. The force of a magnet is strongest at the poles.

You remember that two rubbed balloons push each other away when they are close. This is because two like charges repel each other. Magnets are similar to that. If the north pole of one magnet is close to the north pole of another, the magnets repel each other. If you put a north pole near a south pole, they will pull toward each other.

You can break a magnet into two pieces, and each piece will have a new north and a new south pole. Magnets always have opposite poles.

Earth as a Magnet

Christopher Columbus used a compass to help him cross the Atlantic Ocean. In his time, sailors used compasses, but they did not know why they worked. Around 1600 William Gilbert said that Earth is actually a huge magnet surrounded by a magnetic field.

Similar to small magnets, Earth has two magnetic poles. But the magnetic poles are not exactly at the geographic location of Earth's North and South Poles. They are called magnetic north and south poles.

Scientists are not sure why Earth has a magnetic field. They think the reason involves the melted iron that makes up Earth's outer core. This melted iron moves around as Earth rotates and creates a magnetic field.

magnetic north pole

North Pole

N

South Pole

S

magnetic south pole

The magnetic north pole of Earth is in Canada.
The magnetic south pole is in Antarctica.

Compasses

A compass has a magnet inside it. The magnet is often called the needle. It is attracted to the magnetic north pole of Earth. No matter where you are on Earth one end of the compass needle will always point toward north.

The compass needle points to magnetic north.

This will change if a magnet is placed close to a compass. The pull of the magnet will cause the needle to point to it instead. Because the magnet is so close to the compass, it has a stronger pull than Earth's magnetic north pole.

The compass needle points to the nearby magnet.

Northern Lights

The Aurora Borealis, or the Northern Lights, is a light show in the sky. Charged particles move quickly from the Sun. They are attracted to Earth's magnetic poles. The particles crash into gases in the atmosphere and give off colorful lights.

Electricity Into Magnetism

Electromagnets

In 1820 Hans Christian Oersted was showing how electric current flowed through a wire. Then he saw that a needle on a nearby compass had moved. Oersted realized that a wire with electric current flowing through it creates a magnetic field. The magnetic field around the wire acts as an invisible magnet. This is why the compass needle moved.

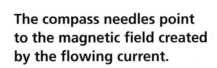

The compass needles point to the magnetic field created by the flowing current.

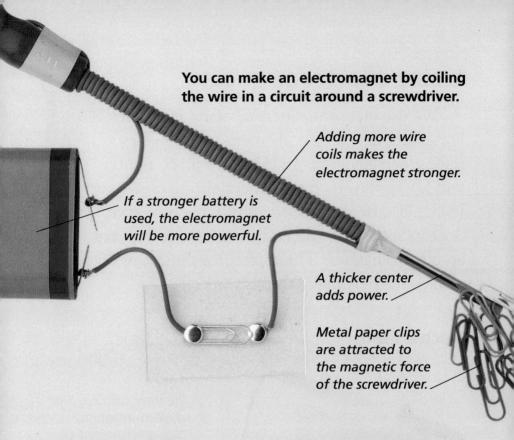

You can make an electromagnet by coiling the wire in a circuit around a screwdriver.

Adding more wire coils makes the electromagnet stronger.

If a stronger battery is used, the electromagnet will be more powerful.

A thicker center adds power.

Metal paper clips are attracted to the magnetic force of the screwdriver.

An **electromagnet** is a coil of wire wrapped around an iron core. When current travels through the wire, an invisible force surrounds the electromagnet. This force is a magnetic field. When you stop the flow of electricity, the electromagnet loses most of its power. Electric energy can be transformed into magnetic energy.

Unlike regular magnets, electromagnets can be made stronger. When you add more coils of wire around the magnet, it becomes more powerful. When you increase the amount of electricity passing through the wire around the magnet, the power of the electromagnet also increases. You can use a bigger magnet or a thicker wire to add to the electromagnet's strength.

Using Electromagnets

We use electromagnets in many machines. For example, vacuum cleaners and blenders have electromagnets in them. So do computers and DVD players. Electromagnets are used in an MRI (Magnetic Resonance Imaging) machine that helps doctors see inside the body. Even a doorbell has an electromagnet! These pictures show how some electromagnets make things work.

electric motor

Battery
This is the source of power.

Rotor
The rotor contains a set of electromagnets.

Commutator
This reverses the direction of the electric current. It makes the north and south poles of the electromagnet flip and causes the motor to spin.

Brush
The brush transfers power to the electromagnet as the motor spins.

Permanent magnet
This works with the electromagnets in the rotor. The north pole of this magnet repels the north pole of the electromagnet. The south poles do the same. This makes the axle spin.

Axle
This holds the commutator and the rotor.

When you press the button, you close the electric circuit. This lets current flow to the transformer.

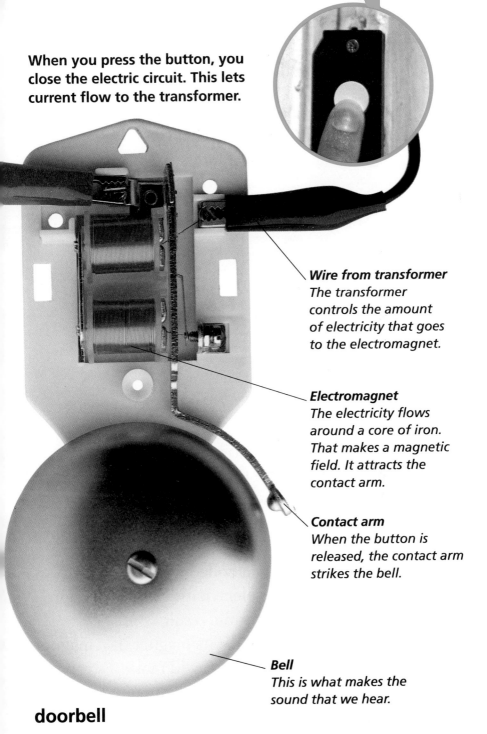

Wire from transformer
The transformer controls the amount of electricity that goes to the electromagnet.

Electromagnet
The electricity flows around a core of iron. That makes a magnetic field. It attracts the contact arm.

Contact arm
When the button is released, the contact arm strikes the bell.

Bell
This is what makes the sound that we hear.

doorbell

Magnetism Into Electricity

Move a piece of copper wire between two magnets to produce electricity.

Electric Energy

We don't often consider how important electricity is to our everyday lives. We turn on lights, televisions, and computers without giving it a second thought. But electricity has come from far away!

We have learned how magnetism can be used to produce electricity. Moving a coiled wire back and forth around a magnet generates electricity. Spinning a wire around a magnet causes the same result.

A magnetic field moves with its magnet. If a magnet or its coiled wire moves quickly, it will make a strong electric current. If the magnet or the wire moves slowly, it creates a weak electric current.

An Early Dynamo

In 1831 British scientist Michael Faraday wanted to use magnets to change motion into electricity. He found that by turning a handle he could produce electric energy. Faraday called this machine a dynamo.

A handle turns a copper disc.

The copper disc spins in the magnetic field.

electromagnet

Currents Today

Most buildings get electricity from generators. A generator makes electricity by turning wire coils around strong magnets. The generators of today are much larger and stronger than those used by Faraday and other scientists. But the basic scientific ideas are the same.

The dynamo turns with the wheel and generates electricity to power the light.

Dynamos can be used for bicycle lights.

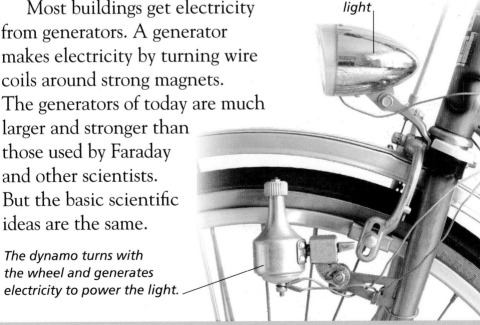

light

Discoveries in Using Electric Energy

600 B.C.

Thales of Miletus describes static electricity.

A.D. 1600

William Gilbert suggests that Earth is a magnet.

1740s

Benjamin Franklin and Ebenezer Kinnersley describe electric charges as positive or negative.

1820

Hans Christian Oersted notices that electric currents affect a compass needle.

1829
1831

Joseph Henry (1829) and Michael Faraday (1831) produce a current by changing a magnetic field.

1870

Zenobe Gramme invents the electric generator.

1879

Thomas Edison demonstrates the incandescent light bulb.

1884

Charles Parsons develops the first successful steam turbine.

1896

Electric generator at Niagara Falls begins producing electricity for Buffalo, New York.

1980

Wind farms in the United States begin collecting the wind's energy.

How Generators Make Electricity

A generator can get its power to make electricity from many sources. It might use steam from a boiler. Or it might use moving water, such as a river. A generator can even get power from the wind or the Sun. Many generators get power from fossil fuels.

Electricity is found in many places. We use it all day for many of the things we do. We see static electricity whenever we see lightning. Electricity and magnetism are closely related. Magnets have a bigger role in our everyday lives than we might realize. Magnets can help generators create electricity. We live on a giant magnet—Earth!

This is a hydroelectric dam. The movement of the water gives power to generators that turn it into electricity.

Glossary

electric current an electric charge in motion

electromagnet a core of iron that is wrapped with a coiled wire carrying electric current

magnetic field an invisible field around a magnet where the force of magnetism can be felt

magnetism a force that can push or pull certain metals that are near a magnet

parallel circuit a circuit in which an electric charge can follow two or more paths

resistance the ability of a substance to resist the flow of an electric charge

series circuit a circuit in which current flows in one path

static electricity the result of positive and negative particles that are not in balance